A BIG and little Alphabet

by Liz Rosenberg
pictures by Vera Rosenberry

ORCHARD BOOKS
NEW YORK

Orchard Books, 95 Madison Avenue, New York, NY 10016

Manufactured in the United States of America
Printed by Barton Press, Inc.   Bound by Horowitz/Rae
Book design by Jennifer Browne

10   9   8   7   6   5   4   3   2   1

The text of this book is set in Goudy Children.
The illustrations are pen-and-ink and gouache reproduced in full color.

Library of Congress Cataloging-in-Publication Data
Rosenberg, Liz.
A big and little alphabet / by Liz Rosenberg ; pictures by Vera Rosenberry.
p.   cm.
Summary: Animals act out verbs beginning with each letter of the alphabet.
ISBN 0-531-30050-1.—ISBN 0-531-33050-8 (lib. bdg.)
[1. Animals—Fiction.   2. Alphabet.]   I. Rosenberry, Vera, ill.   II. Title.
PZ7.R71894Bi   1997   96-53305

For my father and my sister,
the big and little beloveds
who taught me my alphabet

—L.R.

For Maya Troll

—V.R.

A a

Big **A** aims.

Little a aims.

Little b buys
a bike.

Big B buys a bike.

Bb

C c

Little c can.

Big C can.

Big D doesn't dare.

Little d doesn't dare.

D d

E e

Little **e** enters.

Big **E** enters.

F f

Little **f** finds a friend.

Big **F** finds a friend.

Big **G** gets grumpy.

Little **g** gets grumpy.

G g

Hats off to little h! hurray!

Hh

Hats off to Big **H**! Hurray!

I i

Big I is interested in ink.

Little i is interested in ink.

Big **J** jumps.

Little **j** jumps.

J j

Big **K** is kissed by the King.

Little **k** is kissed by the king.

K k

Big L loves little l.

L l

Little l loves Big L.

Little **m** makes mistakes.

Mm

Big **M** makes mistakes.

Nn

Big **N** says no.

Little **n** says no way! nothing doing!

Big O's oak.

Little o's oak.

Big **P** prepares
a pie.

P p

Little **p** prepares a pie.

Big Q is
quiet.

Q q

Little q is quiet.

Big **R** races around.

Little **r** races around.

R r

S s

Big **S** safely suns.

Little **s** safely suns.

Big T triumphs.

Tt

Little t triumphs.

U u

Big U is under an umbrella.

Little u is under an umbrella.

Big **V** vanishes.

V v

Little v
vanishes.

Ww

Little **w**
works.

Big **W**
works.

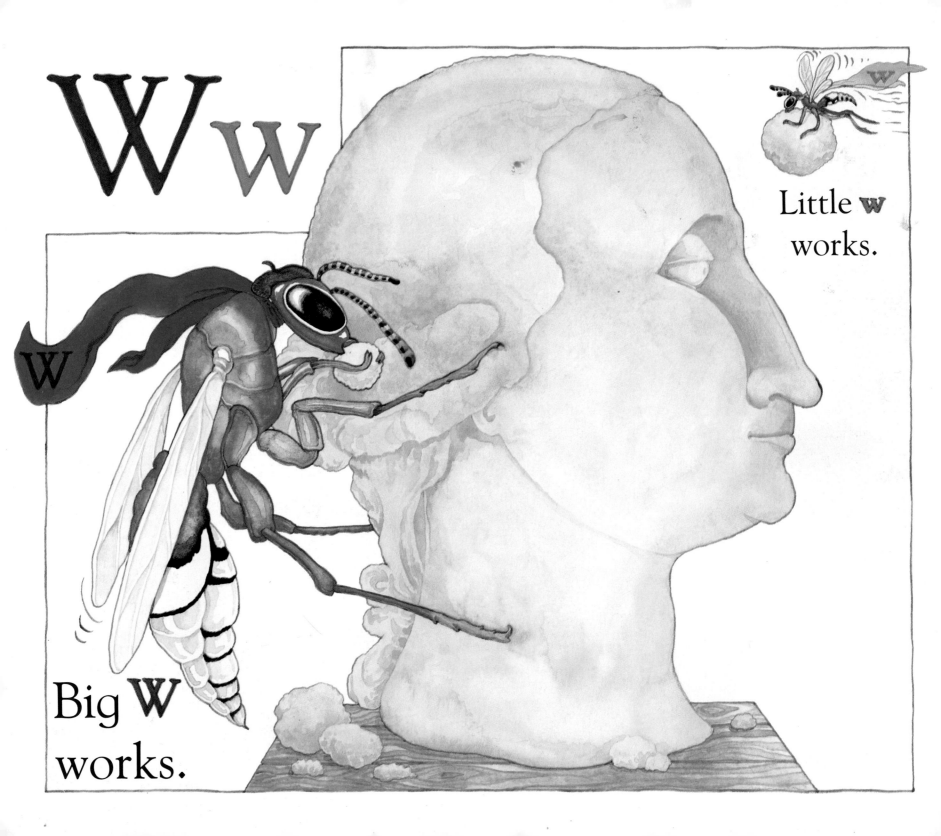

Big **X** gets a bo**X**
(with an a**X**
in it).

X x

Little **x** gets a bo**x**
(with a **x**ylophone).

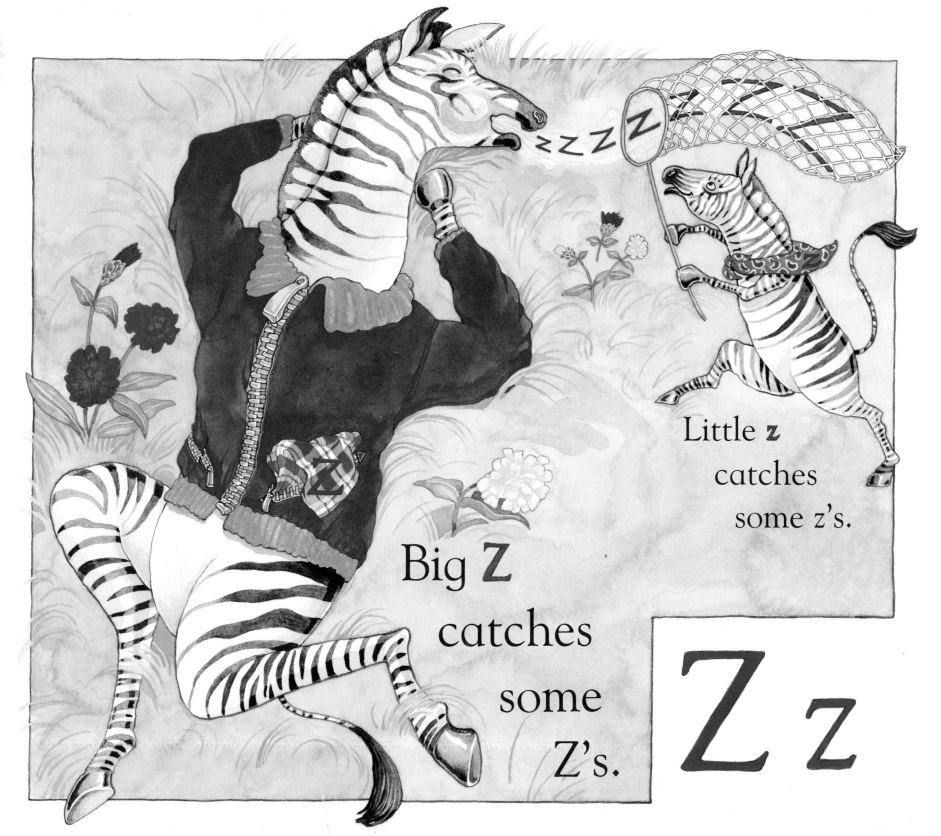

Big **Z** catches some Z's.

Little **z** catches some z's.

Z z

Aa Bb Cc Dd

Ii Jj Kk Ll Mm

Ss Tt Uu Vv

A apple
archery
armadillos
arrows
artichokes

B bears
bees
bicycles
butterflies

C cabbage
camels
candle
candy
canoe
chairs
clock
clowns
coconut
cradle
crate
crow

D deer
diagonals

diamonds
diving boards

E elephants
embroidered vests
exit

F flowers
forget-me-nots
forsythia
frogs
fruit

G garden
geraniums
glasses
goats
gown
grandpa
grapes
grass

H hammock
handkerchief
hats
helium balloons
hippos

hogs
hyacinths

I ibis
ice cream
ink

J jack-o'-lanterns
jacks
jaguars
jesters
jewels
jingle bells
juggling
jugs

K kangaroos
kerchief
king
koala bear

L lace
leaves
lilacs
lilies
lizards
lyre

M map
maze
middy blouses
monkeys
mushrooms

N napkins
narcissus
necktie
newts
noodles
nosegay

O oaks
oboe
owls

P pies
pocket
poppies
porcupines
purple plums

Q quail
quilt

R rainbow
red radio
rhinoceros
rink
roller blades
roller skates

S sand
sandwich
shadows
shells
shovel
snakes
soda
straw
sunglasses

T tassels
tiara
tightrope
tights
torches
trapeze
turtles
tutu

U umbrellas
unicorns

V v-necked ves[t]
vultures

W Washingto[n]
wasps
wig
wings
wood

X ax
foxes
xylophone

Y yaks
yellow mud

Z zebras
zinnias
zippers